(O)

(O)

✠

Sophie Mayer

2015

Published by Arc Publications
Nanholme Mill, Shaw Wood Road,
Todmorden OL14 6DA, UK
www.arcpublications.co.uk

Copyright © Sophie Mayer 2015
Copyright in the present edition © Arc Publications, 2015
Design by Tony Ward
Printed by TJ International, Padstow, Cornwall

978 1908376 98 5 (pbk)
978 1908376 99 2 (hbk)
978 1910345 01 6 (ebook)

Cover image:
Photograph by Tony Ward

This book is in copyright. Subject to statutory exception and to provision of relevant collective licensing agreements, no reproduction of any part of this book may take place without the written permission of Arc Publications.

Editor for the UK and Ireland:
John W. Clarke

CONTENTS

In the Orchard of Pomegranates / 9

I DO

Σοφια / 13
my sister, my spouse / 14
auto-retrato como la casa azul / 15
Effulgent / 16
<phainetai> / 17
Your Tiny Sappho / 18
Lemniscate / 19
Little Red, Riding / 20
The Goblin King's Daughter / 21
Moomins (Mumintroll (Muumi)) b. 1945 / 22
Membrane / 23
Verlören / 24
undone / 25
The Mystique Mutations / 27

I UNDO

Silence, Singing / 33
Phylactery / 41
I am B) / 42
Sonneteratology / 43
Pearl, [what she is] oe'd / 44
Soy_agar.net / 45
Pearl Takes Bronze at the Cultural Paralympiad / 46
An Elegy for the Sonnet as Instrument of Torture / 47
Pearl's Dream of the Daddy State / 48
That Sonnet is an Anagram (Fragmentary) of Constellation / 49
Pearl, Dreaming, is a Tracey Emin Neon Hung at No. 10 / 50
omphalos / 52
Eau d' / 54
Shell Key / 55
Mure/x / 56

David's First Drafts #(3-1=)0: Bathsheba / 58
David's First Drafts #-1: Jonathan / 59
David's First Drafts #∞: God / 60
David's First Drafts #1948: Goliath / 61
Words for It / 62
Observations on Living with a Hole in Your Side / 64
I / 66

I REDO
On Wilds, and Woods / 71
Amiss / 79
Fiona Tan's Saint Sebastian (2001) / 81
Vagina / 82
After Hypatia / 83
Angria / 84
Pissing into the Wind: 2004 / 86
Ostrakoi / 88
All About Suffrage was Taught Under Mrs. Catt's Direction / 89
Penny for Them / 91
Londinos / 92
No Dragons But Fairies / 93
Water-Margin / 95
Pas de deux / 96
Under the same blue sky / 97
Homeric Hymn to Artemis / 98
Where A= ∞ / 100
The Mayer / 101

Biographical Note / 105
Acknowledgments / 107

for S F

we're undone by each other...
and if we're not, we're missing something.

> – JUDITH BUTLER
> *Precarious Life*

IN THE ORCHARD OF POMEGRANATES

> Then you wonder, astonished, who am I? I am a
> mustard seed in the middle of the sphere of the moon.
> Moses Cordovero, *Or Ne'erav* (The Sweet Light),
> trans. Ira Robinson

When I was a girl, holy in sending,
alive in receiving, I knew a word
was, like an angel, flaming, both message
and messenger. Electric the flower

in my eye, the opening of the heart:
if 'house' is a prison, 'home' is a latticed
(look up) constellation. At such elevation
this is return, under you the harvest moon.

Anemone,
anemometer.

I have nothing withheld in my hands, but
nothing. Doubled. The seed of. Your wish for.

I DO

ΣΟΦΙΑ

    search / query –

sapph_

sapphire engagement rings
sapphire and steel
sappho

    sang
    wedding songs

for *beautiful feet* and *a purple girdle*

her girls <ereuthetai>
she says;
    reddening, un-
        graspable,
        the tree's
        last apple

MY SISTER, MY SPOUSE
    KJV Song of Solomon 4:12

we were new eves – school motto : *knowledge
no more a fountain sealed* – at BBC Apples, processing
ourselves at 1000 WPM. touch (type), (key)

stroke: hail! girls-at-arms, hiding *My Secret Garden* beneath
the covers of *The Secret Garden* (or [as per] vice
versa). yes, everything about us clandestine: we were

enigma machines, a clacking Bletchley Park of self-
encoding signals, fingers ever at the red button
of the nuclear heart: clitoral too new (old) a word

for our tongues. we clung, draped, braided, made
up our selves and skins. secretion agents, hand in
glove, hats just-so, belted trenches: we were

parachuted across the lines, packing nylons & eyeliner
(& each other). all that falling silk, all those tiny silver
cylinders we fit into, keys we tried. secretary:

keeper of secrets, locked as in a safe. bars
on the windows so we won't-can't-wish to
fly away; bars where (spies) we pose & honeytrap

(so sweet) our future
       selves: each other.
              synaptically connecting.
     @
             silver tip of your
      studded tongue, open
socket of my lips.

AUTO-RETRATO COMO LA CASA AZUL
self portrait as Frida's house

mi corazón, her corset: the heart of it   *heart*
going hammer and sickle / not sickness
but red silk boots (with lift or prosthesis)

sculptural crutches, slender as brushes
and as necessary: una pasaporte   *passport [to a]*
through each doorway

the flyaway cocina donde   *kitchen where*

calabaza no es cabeza   *pumpkin≠head*
cerdo o cebolla ≠ cerebro // stop   *pig onion≠brain*

thinking in the heart
of the heart, nacreous
or vivid verde (te amo)   *green (i heart you)*

love

how they made the walls
so open, each blue corner
an encuentro: *meeting*
                             beautiful blue
este lengua más bonita de azul,   *tongue*
este laboratorio de ethnographía sensorial

en corazón, razón: tanto = enough   *in heart*
there is, in heart, art   *reason: enough*

EFFULGENT

for Caitlin and Rob

a feasting presence full of light.
WILLIAM SHAKESPEARE, *Romeo and Juliet*, V.iii.89.

or, *Rome(r)o and Juliet*'s lost final scenes, recover'd.

V.iv.

Enter FRIAR *with holy Book, white linens, and tapers alight.*

From the crypt and altar, ROMEO *and* JULIET *arise before him, attended by* PARIS *and* TYBALT, *arisen also, who array* JULIET *and stand witness.*

With these words, he them weds. They kiss.

*

V.v. Epilogue, spoken by THE NURSE

and they, with their lips *warm*,
wed in a kiss, knowing the
poor 'pothecary's potion for what
it is. *restorative*, this scene,
unseen, in which the zombride
gets her Zomeo. together shall be
their spring, their head, their *feasting
presence* in our hearts. and if *the sun
… will not show,* then nights (& days)
savage-wild shall be theirs, of night things
unstopped or -stilled by that pretender,
dawn. *the dearest morsel of the earth* is by holy
kiss between your palms now kindled
full (o light) of light.

<PHAINETAI>

    ἀλλὰ πᾶν τόλματον, ἐπεὶ †καὶ πένητα†...
                             Sappho, Fr. 31

to
 find myself in   that godboy   tonguing her   to laughter
 tied in my skin   tattooed with you   who

skinned yourself senseless at the rose of her   petalshed
left nothing   *nothing for us*
                                                        to do but
                                                       belated

he
 has the words   she leans in   for whispering
                                          bodies is the god's
        last laugh   you steal his fire   hide it

under your skin inked blue *like*   *tattoos* you
know i've been to   see before   eyesburn you
               shimmer   numb
                       and   pulsing

YOUR TINY SAPPHO

from the belly of the wolf
        that streaks across her belly
                in a brush of fur and
            shiver   she
                    calls out   to her own kind
                        a fore(paw)   warning
        of what has come
        between this   skin and its eliminations
                as   (in your element)
you work
        the broken
        alchemist of ruins
elucidating the dark or what is kept

dark, she turns
pages corner-down like sheets
marking your were-here as
starlight candled across her skin
                laid out like
parchment you   brush over   fill in
she will be your tiny sappho
        and call you   her cliff   her hair
                        ribbons long and light enough
to arabesque
each   breathed syllable fading from the mirror
                              opens
              her mouth   moth-kissing
              (note: errata for Stein's *I Am Rose*)
              an error "lips" has been blocked out
              and "eyes" stamped below
        o,   (mark this)
        skin   amanuensis

LEMNISCATE

The King of Swords unlocks his kiss, lip-bruised,
at the last possible instant. Iceburn
at the press of the blade. Oh, at the turn
of the scales, my legs Sheba-haired, tattooed
(hey blue). Snow-licked skin could not be paler
in this wolf season. Dead grass. Poverty.
Pelt and ruff return at a run and free,
under our fingers fleshed deep in her fur.
Shiver Arctic cold or any excuse
to get close. Closer. Yes. As a mouthful
of each other's words, breath, yes. What leaves us
in a kiss is the kiss and all it says
of wonder, windows, eyelids; opening. All
the falling. That tumbled lock. And: chorus.

LITTLE RED, RIDING

Foxes brought her home.
Four at the corners of her coat.
Two at the shoulder, two at the knee.
Foxes brought her home.

                She never felt right in the habit.
         Little Red liked to dress in her own flame hair.
                 She never sat right in the saddle.
         Little Red liked earth at her strong, dark toes.

Foxes cooked her food.
Four it took to catch and to kill.
Two at the henhouse, two at the well.
Foxes cooked her food.

                She never rode right in the canter.
         Little Red took her time to go here and go there.
                She never pulled right on the bridle.
         Little Red yearned for freedom to follow her nose.

Foxes lit her fire.
Four gnawing logs at the woodpile.
Two at the flintstrike, two at the hearth.
Foxes lit her fire.

                Little Red never heeded the hunt horn.
         Little Red liked to sleep in her deep, warm lair.
            Little Red was a girl with a will of her own.
       And now she's a fox and knows what the fox knows.

                   Foxes crossed her dream.
           Little red they were, copper and dun.
           Two at the window, two at the door.
                  Foxes walking through.

THE GOBLIN KING'S DAUGHTER

First sight. Look, I've
said it. Me: medieval, inner eyes open
at conception, receiving an
impression. In the moment
that my ovum opened
to the scenting sperm (don't
roll your eyes, gateways to what
you don't yet know), perhaps I caught
a hint of that mocking laugh: defeat. Half my kingdom
gone, and I knew it –

and, in that knowing, perhaps
he crept, a furtive zygote, turning you
changeling from within. I never told you
what your body knows (its pointed
ears and tufted hair). Your eyes
are his, although (oh no, we
never met again) I think of them as
yours, yes, when you judge me (coldly, just
as he did) for my silence.

You fill me with soft dreams of softness –
our dance in the night, my nose
to the cradle of your skull –
you enrage me with your will (mine, reborn
as magic). How you disappear, how
chaotic you become. How you wind
time (as he could) to suit yourself.

How I would cede my kingdom (all my
little kingdom) to see your smile
reach your eyes.

MOOMINS (MUMINTROLL (MUUMI)), B. 1945

1.

In the morning, it was snowing
umlauts. Points of darkness
fell, swirling in pairs – ash keys;
cartoon eyes – over the valley. Vowels,
suddenly, hesitated, staccato,
in the blizzard, and cried out. Or
tried. Under the blankets, they held
each other. O! and were multiplied.

2.

Words fall into the magic hat
and emerge. Pro- or con-
fusion: uncanny either way. Can't
let talk get fillyjonked: rules must bend
before the storm. In her slang *mymla*: to love
or mumble. What Hattifatteners
(those swarmers) cannot understand.

3.

Here is the news from Moominvalley: Anarchy!
Snoozing! A music festival (hosted by Snufkin)
sounds the things of summer: berries, campfires,
transformations. Tray pancakes and flower-picking picnics
are in. Cascading domestic disasters forecast. Strangers.
Storms. Arctic darkness comes in waves. We hibernate.
And dream in pen-and-ink of – Meanwhile, thunder.

MEMBRANE

&then there were no more tears. We had been
rendered dry-eyed, whatever they fired. Mask, milk,
veil: our eyes open beneath and unblinking. Burn, yes:
at gas and its associations, its membranous insistence.
This us is a skin, a sheath for green or trigeminal;
porous, vulnerable. Shield and: spray of air, hair-fine
and falling as grass-seed. Sown (from slingshot or
peashooter), striking ground and/as galaxy. The hard
skin, the wings: we know this flight (street to street to
street –

And sleep – two sleeps – millions – curled around
– in rocky ground…

Then the rain came (again) and seeds re. Called or
membered: thin and limber, shooting softness into
soil, eating deep earth. Wheat, barley and chickpeas
first brought to hand in fertile: this bedtime tale of
Anatolia. Tulips first grew here, and irises. See(d) our
eyes. In each a tree, and we. Winged and skinned and,
still, unblinking.

VERLÖREN
    after Jem Cohen's Museum Hours

ok, start the journey
here
      outside this cathedral
what's left to pick / is music
(dude, keep playing or they'll bury you)
                              be vulnerable
                              it is no fall /
                                  not a fall
                                  at all   now
                                              come
to the brokenness of time
the dirt that settles on our skin until
                russet ——————— muscle
                      just
                          to hear her sing
            the shifting light
                          the last stars / at grass / these
bird into tree / stone into air
the work in us that / water does
                      our days of metamorphoses

UNDONE

After Athena, she can't stand Parian marble.
The V&A is a chamber of (yes) horror: ghosts
with perfect elbows she wants to sob on. No.
Medusa wants plastic. A backpackful
of trinkets. Hellooooooooooooo Kitty. Hallelujah.
On lonely days, she browses readers
at Silver Moon, but oh, they're
moving marble, bruiseless. Not a skin tone. It's
human. Women turning stone because
she wants them. But it's nothing. They're
not. It's so easier to frieze them. See
how they dance in the courtyard.
Hard mysteries she can't enter. Late at night,
she climbs the moon. Roofwise
London's just a wash, a flash of amber
before dawn's rain or red. She takes a train
out of Paddington but jumps at Reading. Fuck
South. The myth of the beach. Sunburnt her.
Sand in her shoes: the thought of it
glass. *I'm that transparent. Walking on A,
turning my tail in for that set of steak knives.* To be lost
on air when that bitch takes her prince(ss) Perseus
up the aisle. Crude: yes. She's in that kicking mood. Boots
the door open. Walks. London drowns it all out. And a
Walkman, her old one, *The Real Ramona* still a storm,
or the dregs of it. Thundering out, the Thames Basin
so vast the rim's a mystery. Marshes to estuary
to sea. Not what she needs. Tate Modern, new as —
hours queuing for the artist's towers,
those spiral fairytales of stairs: *I Do,
I Undo, I Redo*. Bourgeois spinning gold
from child brides & bluebeards. Her Fimo
miniatures of them, carefully incised,
but the shop won't buy. 'Come back

after your first solo show, OK?' – she throws
them into the maw of the river & follows them
downstream, bridge after bridge, past Greenwich,
her sketchbook banging at her back. If she turned
inland, there would be Dulwich, where. With Athena.
Feminist angels & their flaming swords amid Palladian
cricket. No, she turns back, haunts the South Bank;
spends late summer sitting on the rough wooden carvings
outside the National Film Theatre. Makes herself sick
with cheap white wine, palms books (overpriced):
Women's Press SF with its black/white spines. Lesbian
planets, lesbian vampires, lesbian aliens & their
vibrators. Sends the book to Athena. No note. Postcard
of Bourgeois' *Spider*. Wishes, as she leaves the Post Office,
that she'd kept it. Too late. A gift's a gift. Intention's
all. When A doesn't write back, she won't
(take to the skies with the female man) be undone.

THE MYSTIQUE MUTATIONS

    I.

Every night I will be
who you want
from me: the secret skin
beneath the scales, the one he
gave me: memory. His imprint in
my DNA. He will be there
in my mind as we
learn each others'
limits. Even if he is not
in yours he will be
in your arms.
Shall I show you?

    II.

He lit a candle
in you that you want
to snuff. Wax soft
as a childhood
shimmer: memory. His image in
your eye as it turns
to me. I am not your diamond
girl, but soft (as fur is
soft) as wax. Impress me
with what you want
of him: push it into me
like a coin. Reversed, I
will wear him
as an emblem. Shall
I show you?

III.

'Go with him,' he said,
'I know it's what you want.' Wrong. Can't
read me: what I wanted was him
to beg. To want me
as he wanted you: you
whom he wants so much
he gave you
me, to be
the conduit between
you open
always: a wound, a small
shattering at which you
break. Remember: I'm your mirror,
the glass between
the two of you through which
you see each
other, unsilvered. Shall I
show you?

IV.

If the Beast were the Beast really, and I
his Beauty, some magic
mirror would show
the life we left behind: him
pacing the castle. Me caught
in a hall of choices, a
shattering of faces, facets, assets
he says I should hide
under my skin (where I kept
him and you

find him out with your touch, oh
all I wanted is all)
you want. Fingers gentle
at temple, his impossibly pink
lips, the kiss
catching us in a stopped moment. X. Mark it
with your tongue
caught rough on my scales
and that tune vibrates
in him, his promises broken
and unbroken: yes, I invite him
in as (I invite) you (did). Paralysed
by his desire he braces, sighs
inside his spiderweb of pain
and want. He feels
that he can no longer feel but
he is oh so
tender as you enter me
and I know you
feel it too: his bliss
that passes vengeance
through us. He is still
our home: you
live in him, come
home to him, nothing
can hide your eyes. Shall I show
you?

v.

and where am I in this
Versailles of wanting? Nothing
I can show you comes close

to his power, and mine
is to be
other. Whatever
this skin thing
is, it is between
us: we cannot
cross it
for all our x'ing.
You think
in me you've found some
blue truth, immutable, some mark
of knowing what you hold. Even I
don't know how deep this surface, how
much I might change
into who you cannot touch. Yes,
I might slip this skin, can live
in anyone, in any other, in
anonymity. Who wears a uniform
of difference? I've seen your
style, your taste of metal, your
rain of death. I've seen your plans
undone. It's time.
Shall I show you
mine?

I UNDO

SILENCE, SINGING

These are the words I was given.
    Be a good daughter.
    Lead a good life.
    Find a good husband.
    Be a good wife.

It was the first poem anyone had ever written for me: my grandmother inscribed it in my bat-mitzvah present, an Artscroll machzor, the prayer book for the High Holydays.

*

In my matching Artscroll *siddur*, I could have found this short prayer said daily: 'Blessed are you, Lord our God, Ruler of the Universe, who has not made me a woman.'

Not that I would have been in synagogue for weekday morning prayers: as a woman, my presence couldn't count towards *minyan*, the quorum for prayer, and I couldn't wear *tefillin*, the phylactery that literally ties God's word to the skin.

*

Now I have escaped the binds of a 'life' chiming only with 'wife,' what I see in the inscription is, paradoxically, how I learned to escape: the powerfully profane act of handwriting, on a holy book, a prayer of your own.

*

I had precedent.

Mary Sidney Herbert, Countess of Pembroke, is one of the earliest known female poets in English, and one of the first women to translate sacred texts into the vernacular. After the death of her brother, Sir Philip Sidney, she continued his work on a metrical translation of the Book of Psalms, including Psalm 130, the famous 'De profundis clamavi.'

Translation is a kind of mutation. Like Mystique, Mary Sidney slips into the skins of a series of men. Not only her brother, but also other English translators of the Psalms: Thomas Wyatt, George Gascoigne, Thomas Sternhold, William Whittingham.

And behind them, King David, legendary lover / fighter, conqueror poet, to whose bloodied hand and honeyed tongue the Psalms are attributed.

With his tongue in her mouth, Mary Sidney is seeking a solution of her own: at once poem and prayer.

*

The opening of her translation of 130 sets out the stakes:
>   From depth of greif
>   Where droun'd I ly,
>   Lord for releife
>   To Thee I cry:
>   my ernest, vehment, cryeng, prayeng,
>   graunt quick, attentive, heering, waighing.

Prayer or poem, it's speech from, and in, profound need: of a listener.

*

As Anne Carson argues in her essay 'The Gender of Sound,'

no-one likes to hear a woman's 'vehment, cryeng' – which is too often how women's writing is apprehended. Confessional, over-emotional, nonsensical, hysterical. But Mary Sidney insists that 'cryeng' is also 'prayeng,' a protestation of the individual relationship with God – or, in a secular sense, the right to be speak and be heard.

If the life others have prayed for you is 'wife,' how can you demand that right?

*

From the depths – *mima'amakin* in Hebrew – a new language forms. What cannot be articulated invents, in its urgency, new articulation. Perhaps you need that new language because you're at the limits of where good behaviour can take you: 'greif,' or rage, or desire, or their meeting point.

'De profundis' was the title posthumously given Oscar Wilde's famous letter from prison, one it shares with dozens of poems in the European canon.

*

Elizabeth Barrett Browning, another precedent for squaring the circle of being a (good) girl and being a poet, wrote a 'De Profundis' after the death of her husband. In it, she says: 'I knock and cry, – Undone, undone!'

Here we are at the edge of language: 'undone,' a word that undoes itself. It speaks its unspeakability. It dares to unlace the corset of good behaviour.

*

Thomas Wyatt also used Psalm 130 to comment on the limits of good behaviour. It's likely he translated it between his arrest on allegations of adultery with Anne Boleyn in 1536 and his death in 1542.

He translated it as part of the sequence known as the Penitential Psalms, supposedly written by David after he had his lover Bathsheba's husband murdered. Murder (not to mention both sexual and military conquest) is the murky depth from which David prays.

Yet David's account of his seduction of Bathsheba – like his defeat of Goliath the Palestinian, and subsequent conquest of Palestine – is still told, and heard, as a boast, not penitence.

*

Wyatt opens Psalm 130:
> From depth of synne, & from depe dispayre
> Fro depth of deeth, fro depth of hart's sorowe
> Fro this depe caue, of darkenes, depe repayre
> The haue I called (O Lorde) to be my borowe

*

Wyatt calls on God 'to be [his] borowe' – a convenient rhyme for sorrow, but one that implies a curious relationship between the speaker and his listener.

Mary Sidney seeks 'attentive, heering, waighing.' Using the present participle, Gertrude Stein's favourite part of speech, she implies reciprocity. Wyatt, though, is cutting a deal.

The OED cites his line for the word's obsolete definition

as a noun: 'borrow, of persons: A surety, hostage; bail, deliverer from prison.' He's looking for God to bail him out.

*

Borrow is first found as a noun in the Laws of Aethelred in 1000. The medieval poets Rolle and Langland use it with the spelling 'borgh[e]' to mean a pledge or loan. It derives from the Old German *berg-an*: to protect, shelter, to shut in. Berg-an leaves its trace in the words borough, burgher, bourgeois, and Borgen; also burrow, bury, and burial.

The walls that shelter us will also wall us in.

Not Wyatt, though. Even in prison, but he knows he's good for a loan from the God zone. In the depths of grief, he turns glibly to the language of power, money and law. Status: quo.

*

I was brought up to believe that my body was borrowed from (in ascending order) husband, father and God; rights in it passed directly from the last to the latter to the first. There were no words I could own, or in which to own myself.

*

A girl stands at the edge of an armed camp, at the edge of the sea. Usually turbulent, they have both fallen still. A suspended hush. Like Bathsheba's, her body is the pivot of a war, subject of a king's law. It is a borrow.

One story says that before she was born, her father the king offered a god the most beautiful thing he saw that year.

Another source says the god demanded a sacrifice before a king could go to war against his Eastern neighbours.

Most sources say nothing at all. About her, Iphigenia.

The Furies' judgement on her brother's revenge for her mother's vengeance for her murder at her father's hands will become, in Aeschylus' account, the foundation of the Athenian state, the buried secret at the heart of law.

She is the borgh[e], berg-an, the invisible security on which our myth of democracy stands.

*

Euripides wrote two plays about Iphigenia. They are our main source for her story, and he told it backwards: in the first play, *Iphigenia among the Taurians*, she is alive and the war is over. The god that wanted her dead has saved her.

Artemis 'translates' her from under her father's knife, substituting a deer. A priestess of a death cult in Tauris, Iphigenia cures and saves her vengeance-maddened brother so they can return to Athens – and the Furies, who will rule her murder insufficient cause for her mother's revenge.

*

The sacrifice happens offstage in *Iphigenia at Aulis*, Euripides' final, bleakest work. The limits of his language.

The only evidence for Artemis translation here is a messenger's speech to Clytemnestra, or rather a fragment of it cited in an obscure grammar book, not present in any other surviving text of the play. Some critics argue Euripides didn't finish it before he died. Couldn't.

There are no facts on the ground; the incompossible versions are entangled with the untanglable knot of Iphigenia's sacrifice and its necessity. If she dies, then vengeance, then law. If she is saved, then vengeance, then law.

*

After all the words for kill, there is a silence. In the silence, singing. 'Vehment, cryeng' that men do not want to hear.

In *Agamemnon,* Aeschylus has the Watchman tell the Chorus that Iphigenia tried to sing when she was brought to the altar. He says that she had sung prayers at her father's table. Who knows, says the Watchman, what curse she would have called down had they not gagged her.

From the depths, she cries out. Undone, undone.

*

The cry and the knife: we know which cuts the silence.

A history in which Iphigenia is allowed to sing – in which her song changes her ending – is not the history we live in. And yet (listen) it is.

*

There is no unwriting Iphigenia's death. But there is writing it: borrowing it, not to shore up the security of the status quo, but to graffiti the walls. Not to uphold the law, but to break it.

We are listening – 'quick, attentive, heering, waighing' –
at the limits of hearing, between his lines, for her song.
Being undone, she (in silence) sings.

PHYLACTERY

gOd my mouth used to hold
your water. A vase I was (say:
vessel) all floral-spoked
& speaking: pure pure pure
as law. This
    knuckle clavicle
mouthful
chewed & throated to you. Choker,
much. Narrow as they say &
swallow.

o my mouth
    knuckle clavicle
unholds your water,
sweet source. Loosener,
marsh-runner, our lady of
statuary hung among
trees. Chatelaine of strange
fruit & the bloodied tunic. Kill me
now, before I turn, before
I fly. I
    knuckle clavicle
mouth an O
cannot no
let him leave me
from you. No
nock me, fingers
to my fletch, for
everyourgirl, prayerful this
fall & broken no
   knuckle
   clavicle that I am no woman no
dawn gives (thirteen times &) thanks

I AM B)

& have my father's feet: necrotten
roots of a leafless stumpy tree. Chipped
as the old block, they're medieval
potatoes, the warts in a Breughel.
Bosch's hell, complete with carbuncles.
An Archimboldo of broken toes,
a foot fetishist's Picasso. Rough
enough to pumice concrete. All my
stupidities made chalky matter –

> Literally oedipal, I stumble
> over my own. It's a total mouthful,
> psychoanalysis, bone of intent-
> ion. Broken. Broken. Rhymes with unspoken.
> Ankylosing. Ankle-losing. Plantar
> fasciitis. 'Muscular' politics. Fuck this
> attempt at balance, this *vrksasana*
> entitlement to earthy rootedness /
> crowning liberties, to karmic cupcake
> ground from bidden fruits. If tree then blasted
> eucalypt that lies while standing, that sucks
> facts from the (humus) ground. Leaches, bleaches.
> Stolen olive branch barbed-wired & greenlined,
> not mine but mined. Particularities:

shattered navicular, phalanges
set at hunchback angles, hangnails and
chiropodic gallows humour. Dirt
inheritance in a chest of bone.
What I have to stand on. Broken. Ground.

SONNETERATOLGY

This ooze is us: the tilting city of us visible
in its shunting, in its melismas. Who cast us
in clear resin, jarred us, until here we are: dis
splayed. Mutated to meet the needs of
a poisoned world. Gill to gill we dance,
my crutch pressed up between your prostheses,
the necklace of my tumours tangled
in your iridescent locks. What prophetic tango
our skin speaks, our nifty six fingertips (light
at loom or touchscreen, equally). My squally
darling, my freak-show embryo: we will drag
ourselves over the slivers. Spike our cha-cha heels
with them, rim each orifice with shards of glass.
And glitter. And glitter. And. And glitter.

PEARL, [WHAT SHE IS] OE'D

> Here and there gold Oaes 'mong Pearls she strew.
> IZAAK WALTON, *Chalkhill's Thealma & Clearchus*,
> cited in OED, o n.3, 2b

Though oe'd and spangled in the gawdiest tyre
her gaping, open mouth (more commonly)
th'O – o, egg of ever – is obsolete.
Is margarite, oocyte of origins
unknown, not non-pareil: pupil of eye
its lesions; of letter size is least, as
of ash & bitter pills. Gelatinous,
onomastic: practical extraction
slash virtual stash. Bovine TB will
hash packets, clarify sugar to moth
millet fritillary or nautilus.
O adjectival, distinguishing mark,
opacity. Blank blank of cataracts,
look me up: a cipher, a mere nothing.

SOY_AGAR.NET

> The surreal nightmare of internationally-acclaimed artist and professor Steve Kurtz began when his wife Hope died in her sleep of heart failure. Police who responded to Kurtz's 911 call deemed Kurtz's art suspicious and called the FBI.
> From the website for *Strange Culture*,
> Lynn Hershman Leeson's film about Kurtz' case

Oh poetry. The state is yr petri dish and – strange cultured –
you multiply. No enemies but bacteria. All emergent,
you are. Excess. Replicative. Terpsichorean. For all the carbon
density. They – we – are *ensemble*. Reaching critical. Feeling
      for the art.
Beat. That silence before. Steve (say, Saint Eve) arrested
in his garlanded Not-Eden. Lynn turns her camera
on him. Or clones. La Swinton neither. Alive nor.
Eaten. See, a need to talk about 'the weather'. That it's
coming, isotopical. Where we are monocultured
by chemicals. New & mercurial, a language that does *not*
occupy, idles no more, that scrounges where found un/
fit to shirk. Things grow in the medium (soy agar with 5%
sheepsblood). Things you can find online. Proliferative
they love. Cellular, uncarbonate, this life thing, desiring.

PEARL TAKES BRONZE AT THE CULTURAL PARALYMPIAD

Cast (before swine, of course): models, accessible,
of all the Tate Turbine Hall installations. Bourgeois'
stairs Stannah'd; those Höller slides all rails and Braille;
Eliasson with audio narration. Myself as the Crack,
Salcedo's *Shibboleth* running right through. And the judges,
callow, ask, 'How did she do it?' to the uneven
cold concrete of each hemi-brain. Forgive me
my callous callosum, my corpus more zomboid
than superhuman. Welcome to the wetland, where
– meddled – 'Olympic Gold Meadows' grow:
sheaves and sheaves awaiting harvest. Lo, Atos win
the contract for the scything. Suits them. And this
heavy metal suits me: consider me bronzed, fifth
plinthed with Lapper, our flippers and nodules
rendered *immortelles* in cold-cast pigeonshit. Dig in,
precious, it's what makes things grow: grit or shit,
petri or endometrium. Not dead and gold, not
dead and gold.

AN ELEGY FOR THE SONNET AS INSTRUMENT OF TORTURE

So, Wyatt, you felt guilty, did you? Guilt dribbling
down the line of your body like
come leaking from your courtier mouth. You
didn't swallow. Couldn't. What was the etiquette,
then, anyway, amidst the farthingales and codpieces?
Did your tongue dance a volta
with the clitoris of the king's mistress?
HBO says so, but TV's a reliable guide to fuck-all,
and certainly not to fucking. But there's a Tudor
Kama Sutra not quite encoded – I'm certain, and who's
to contradict me – in Shakespeare's sonnets
and in yours: a diagrammed manual
of swan's-wing hair torture, needle-pricked
play piercing, studded collars, whip-smart naked hunts,
cockringing, double blind-
folds, precise stiletto stabs to the breast and groin. Oh, how
you all loved torture, falling under it, tumbling
to the enseamèd bed for a thumbscrew. Our inheritance
from you: a mouthful of crown jewels,
a snail trail of slipped identities and dirty linen,
all buckled to a verse form that plays
daisy chains with rhymed pairs (legs
entwined in exquisite crucifixions),
whose ecstatic utter shudder is its
quietus: auto-poetic asphyxiation.

PEARL'S DREAM OF THE DADDY STATE

> Perle, plesaunte to prynces paye
> To clanly clos in gold so clere.

It is inside me, spidery. Fistsized, throatlump
lumping outwards: black birth. All these questions
that are not. Choker of Arial Bold with misplaced
apostrophe's. Name. Age. Sex. Diagnosis. Yes. No:
bureaucratic ink shelobing up my maps. I die
in the desert that wasn't there. No signal, however
shined my coltan. Beep. Each day I am summoned
to attend the court, where green-gloved
judges operate on tumours with their golf clubs. Shunt.
The witness box is not 'grandfathered' under
laws on accessibility. To testify, therefore, I lie
on the jury bench while the gavel strikes.
The jury (you guessed it) is arachnid, hirsute
and malevolent in corners. The chips are down
& the Minister for Roulette, Soviet style,
announces new production targets (yawn,
change the channel, [don't] see it coming) in the sector
(outsourced) for mortality. Sow and reap. In the frame,
Pearl leans on her scythe, every inch the rural
fantasia: Wordsworth girl, rickets and severed
fingers invisible. So pierce me: I am landfill
indie, sob story, Remploy contracted
to cold-cast Pierrots with a single tear. Kiln
those cherubs and their gilty wings. In the parade
at the gates, I-I-I-I am threaded on every spoke;
crushed to dust, aglitter in every cast, every glass
eye; ball-and-socketed, old hip
for new. For I. Am. Pearl: grit dis-
ease of seabed shirkers, nacreous pill unsleeping
beauty. Useless jewel.

THAT SONNET IS AN ANAGRAM (FRAGMENTARY) OF CONSTELLATION

O Marlene on the wall: I made you
the angel of your own night sky, glow
(in the dark) brighter than city stars (glitch
-ing streetlights) and closer. Flashbulb celebrity
nebula ready for close-up, the moon's circum-
ference measuring up to a meteor's, similar
to Saturn's. You're encircled by this yearning
to lift the roof & be in among the weather
of the (that [real]) world: walls fall, nightmare
papier mâché melts to let in something stranger –
cat-footed – that holds its breath and stalks
my hurting heart. Oh Marlene, among (other) stars,
you're no comfort now: light can travel so far
(only) in the time we have to live (here) in the dark.

PEARL, DREAMING, IS A TRACEY EMIN NEON HUNG AT NO. 10

> So women are maintained at a distant/inferior position to be psychically milked, much the same way ants maintain colonies of aphids to provide a life-giving substance for their masters.
> AUDRE LORDE, 'The Uses of the Erotic,'
> *Sister Outsider*

My cunt, I say, is (pinkly) wet with fear. I am electric
kitty passed through neon sealed in a kinked glass. Hanged,
I am, in halls of power. This house of cards for
le cadavre exquis. At night – that is, each night – he comes
up to my door. The keyhole, its aperture, makes his penis
hard. Unyielding, makes him harder. It makes him
rage. He is in the room, then, every night: naked, a presence,
malevolent. Eight legs: a compensation for some
lack. His many hands about my neck, between my legs.
In the wet. Dissolve. This is no dream. By day, he's all
princes, and all states I: his settled colony, enclosure, domain,

    king's ransom: where once were eyes, areolae. Nub: coin of
        his realm

> (nb: J. Polidori, *Journals (1816)*:
> L.B. repeated some verses of Coleridge's **Christabel**, *of the witch's breast; when silence ensued, and Shelley... looking at Mrs S.... suddenly thought of a woman he had heard of who had eyes instead of nipples, which, taking hold of his mind, horrified him)*

my flesh. All duty, paid. But what (more) – tea leaves
on the water – can a body do? *This* is a dream: every night he.
By ways and means, erases. As textbook, heart-throb, figure
in the carpet. It's all textu(r)al, up-stitching me. Blinding
labour, unfair trade: my lustre tarnished as his crown's
enhanced. Or: what an irritation I must be.

His need for me. That cavity in him where I sit. It is   no
compensation for his tearing of me, that little living death.

But I learned some whip-sting from my jellyfish
sister. She whispers, cnidocytically, *tonight leave your door
open*. Oceanic, viscocity will *lap about you. We are
with you, in the flood, the gush of us:* ugly, gelatinous and
tentacular, luminescent, swallowing & unswallowing *our
own skin : your kin your kin*. Your kin. Open your door, your
too-small aquarium. The phosphorescent sea is come
& he – needful of darkness, coward of the shadows,
silence scrounger, locked-door dependent – he is fled.
My cunt: yes, still wet, & still   with fear.
I own it and (as) the krill-pinked ocean, kinked
with my sister's neon scribbles flashing
        OPEN   OPEN   OPEN

OMPHALOS

> this, then, is the navel of the dream, the place where it straddles the unknown
> SIGMUND FREUD, *The Interpretation of Dreams*,
> trans. Samuel Weber

Stolen, the dream image: table
laid *à deux* mid-swimming pool (tectonic semaphore
from Venice). In evening dress. My elemental
brilliantined teacher, beekeeper
keener on solitary flight than hivemind, curative curate
in human drag, never quite – Watch those square-
tipped nails, those catgut lines, catching light
to throw it: not as shadow but. Dream now older
than its dreamer was then, who was
no-one's Tadzio. Who was not
his. Who steals this (from myself) for solace. Still
watching.

*

It's a fantasy [*sparagmos*]: not the clumsy
thrust unbuttoning of human thumbs all thumb but some
tearing that could release. Please! one cannot claw
one's own ⎯⎯ out. Oh please fill
the blank that settles in as skin.

What will fold will fold will.

Leadhour (if out) on the flat black
terminal. Stars are sisters protected
witnesses re & renamed against. Still waiting still.

*

Motorway headlight glow,
soughing of night wheels, ghost
of the window. Lives and lives
past, lives over the meridian
and into darkspace, 'country'
'shire.' Night this: and memory
of nights, heart pulling back
to the conurbation, that lick
at tears, that. Neckback, drift,
roll, glare. Air of driven. All over
the place is place, is a silverlilac
subtle sky, and. City, limits.
The edge that's lived, and inner,
chilly arrow fletched – still – in bright,

EAU D'

Stream this.

*

Hydration a transaction: liquid assets crossing borders (semi-permeable). The nation's plasmolysed: supplies like glass spheres suspended. And smash to splinters.

*

In this season of drought come floods.

*

In this the puddle it is possible to drown. So rumour rivers and denies its source. Thus spake Echo, her name a desert. A drowning pool that fills my throat with your reflection.

*

The luxury I piss away, I also weep.

SHELL KEY

yoho, as the shanties go, she'll selkie
she sells sea she she'll sound sure
bells for her, alert to x second of
extinction / wait, label this nothing
official or, orificial: opening
an evidence; say, artifice
(du feu) in pinks prinked & frilled
little grisette with a wicked grille
has shrugged off her grisaille
with a leg & a knife & what seems
silence (listen, a salt whisper to scour
the ear) she's not here for <u>that</u>,
this girl is (not) for sale, neither *sale*
nor *salé*, a salopette all bucket no spade
thus stranded, sablé (source: Sévigné),
she's a rich bitten biscuit, teethmarks
an occam mock-up – simple as ____ ,
sweet as _____: there's no way to
read this 2D into hap, fingers caught
napped at the undertow – chaotic! all your
wave forms on a spiral to infinitude
her *attitude*: say, lip & pull it,
all the 'twixts she cups between
within & wouldn't you like to know
o!, as the old shanties go, she'll
sell you sea, as much as the shell
of your two hands can carry

MURE/X

walled up in the purple
birthing chamber (how
byzantine) I am shelled
shell dyed die inedible
treasure (its price above
rubies) rubescent wealth
of the cedars (sc. caesars)
synagogue fathers in ((*shul*)) shawl
and secret the indigo isle
indignant or dayglo with
artisan calibans knitting
fish scales to fall for
tourists' eyes (how golden
fleeced they'll be, ship their
long Phoenician oars, their
alpha and their o
daiyenu

enough

already to say *croceus*:
pricey soft stems (called
stigma)) picked in sunlight
by women's fingers (mustn't
bruise or lose the precious
dust) subject of the Trojan
trade war: colour of kingly
carpets, of Helen's hair,
crocuses of the Troezen
rubbed to bright blood
embroidered on shrouds
with thread dip-dyed in
saffron threads that bind
in Sappho's poem (her name

a fragment of the gold)
al-zafaran whose songs
could stop the plague
whose colour carried over
and dyed the darkening sea

DAVID'S FIRST DRAFTS #(3-1=)0: BATHSHEBA

Fuck you, Bathsheba,
and your little dog, too. You're not
invited to this party. Sorry,
off the list.
> *Off the chart, the ecstasies*
> *of your hair, the scars*
> *it left.*

You can't come
in, only pour: out out out. You leak.
You stink of the farmyard.
And the docks.
> *Let me dock in you (once,*
> *twice) in the close-*
> *openness of your dark.*

Enough with the wailing
and the mascara trails. You look
like a whore, always did. That's right:
what I wanted was easy.
> *Wanting was easy with you*
> *It's easy wanting, easy*
> *to want. There's nothing in life but you.*

And you fucked it up. He fucked
it up. He died and left you
a widow. Holy of holies: a woman
who has flown the trap of man.
> *And I couldn't —*
> *couldn't enter*
> *the beauty of your solitude.*

So take your god-damned freedom
and get far from me. You take
it wrapped in silk, be its priestess, call upon me to worship its
    absence, the absence,
oath's daughter, I always wanted.

DAVID'S FIRST DRAFTS #-1: JONATHAN

Fuck you, Jonathan. You
abandoned me.
What was it you said? Oh yes: *our love
is too beautiful for this world*. Fuck you.

Nothing, Jonathan, nothing
is too beautiful
for this stupid, unruly world &
don't roll your eyes & ask
if I'm alive to the ambiguity. I'm the poet-king & nothing,

beautiful Jonathan, nothing is more
beautiful in my eyes
than you, so I cling, I cling with my
filthy bitten
fingernails to your non-existence, beautiful

filthy bitten sight – Jonathan – seen
everywhere
in the nowhere that passes
the ark
as it passes. I'm the drunken filthy

poet-king, Jonathan, that Plato saw in nightmares
dancing naked
in this gaping, ragged hole
that is power.
I'm naked without you, not a poem but a king,

Jonathan, that is power & I
hate it. Tell me how he did it, your father,
& why I wanted it more
than I wanted you, my king-poem, my Jonathan.

DAVID'S FIRST DRAFTS #∞: GOD

Fuck you, God, All Father. Ashamed
of you how made me, are you,
with the swing of my balls, here
before your Covenant: look, the root
of multiplication.

Take it in hand, my Lord,
All Fluffer, open sky-mouth
and suck me down to cosmic
howl. O world turned up
side down and all that's
David isn't to be so undone.

You designed this latch
at the mid of us, O Lord,
All Faller, this covenanted ark
that cries forth 'Our Failer who
art in every hole & calls it
heaven.' Drunken shudder under Jerusalem
skin. No walls can stand it
(that's why we build 'em to keep this shudder in).

So when I say 'Fuck you, God, All
Fucker,' I mean it: the messy bed of heaven,
my flesh&genitals interpenetrating
your skycloudbody, all hole and burning
skin until we cry, together, 'O Lord' & in doing

your own undoing
the world ceases
for a second when
all hearts come
clean as a psalm.

DAVID'S FIRST DRAFTS #1948: GOLIATH

Oh you huge stone
butch if only I
could have

                              put off the shepherd
                                  boy the sheep
                                      the herd

                                  my skin my king
                                  hood cast aside
                                    that breech
                                        clout

                                  stood naked in
                                    this greater
                                      power

touched
                                          love

you

Gymnos

To slip the sullied flesh, in lycra cut so low as to reveal: sharp ells of shoulder blades, s of scoliotic spine.

It is the art of naked, a stretch in skin: the limit, addictive, of embodiment.

To be a girl is not to be girl: it is not to be. To be not (me) (not) the body a girl's condemned to be.

Pranayama

It starts with breath. With the breath. With a. And again, and. Stoma, cilia, alveoli. What we know of blood is breath, its beating at the chest that says

IcantIcantI.

Pullbacking all that surfaces as tension. Yokes strength and loss: the holding that will not be held. They say: breathe into. (o) in the machine.

Ru'ach

Holey: blown through: all matter is. Space, and what is not is this, thing; spirit. Written on forehead, scroll between my lips.

I carry ancestors (no metaphor) on that holy breath of naming: two women, pre-photographic. Blacks & silks beyond the pale.

By any other name is flesh, & flesh is matter, & matter gaps. It lacks it lacks it lacks. No animation, no antic, no an, no a.

Corpus

> compulsion stops.
>   John Kinsella, 'Burning Eyes'

Found in a cradling: the ribs a rush basket for the unnamed knot. Swaddled if uncertain. Sailed on the red river of systole//diastole//stop.

Gasp. Stop. Gasp. Utter. St–utter it. Stop it. Like you mean it, bitch. Tripped over the halt of itself. A sign language unassigned, spoken in flush at edges. Stop.

And ragged 'go,' in sobs torn against the grain for collaging: some new bone, boiled, to hold it all, to turn the blank wall into everything, a skin of everything.

Beneath which: the uninsulated hollow whistling with the rips. Still this. The hole that's all I have. The curve flexed at emptiness. Start as –

OBSERVATIONS ON LIVING WITH A HOLE IN YOUR SIDE

1.1

Being the Son of God
makes it no easier: no less
painful, no less unhealed.

1.2

Everyone will want
to touch it. Everyone.
Especially those who deny its existence.

1.3

You will want to touch it,
too. To feel the sting and seep
that says, incredibly, you are alive.

2.1

Being the son of Mary
makes her tears no easier: her gasp,
her soothing hands that cannot stanch this wound.

2.2

Everyone will want
it shrouded. Everyone.
Especially those who were there & saw the damage done.

2.3

You will want to shroud it,
too. To smoothe the sore (that once was skin)
that says – humans are this: violent, this cruel.

3.1

Being, humankind, the son of Man
makes it. No: easier with the pain,
the tears, the gasp of unwanted recognition.

3.2

Everyone will want
it. To remain yours, not theirs.
Especially not theirs. Nor ours. Not mine.

3.3

You will want to not want it,
too much. Addictive. The wound
       that says, inaudibly. I am not you. I. I am.

I

this is a poem in which there is a silence

    the silence is a quotation

    the quotation is from *Agamemnon,* a play written in 458 B.C.E.

    the play is about a woman murdering a man

    the woman's murder is predicted by another woman: a mad woman

    the mad woman will not be silent, she remembers

    the remembering happens to everyone except the man who is to be murdered: he has forgotten

the forgotten thing is:

    And on her lovely mouth –

to check the cry that would have cursed his house –
he fixed a bridle....
for she used to sing to them around her father's table,
blessing their libation in her pure girl's voice –

what happened then I did not see and cannot tell.

    the telling is done in these words by Anne Carson, two and a half centuries after the silencing

    the silencing is a curse, and is full of curses

the curse is these lines, spoken by a watchman
       ten years after the man murders his daughter;
       a thousand lines later, the knife falls on him: the
       knife the watchman didn't see, the knife the
       man raised on his daughter

the daughter is alive in the silence

the silence is the poem

I REDO

ON WILDS, AND WOODS

> Impatient of a yoke, the name of bride
> She shuns, and hates the joys, she never try'd.
> On wilds, and woods, she fixes her desire
>   Ovid, *Metamorphoses*, Book I,
>   translated by John Dryden

līber free < the same Indo-European base as ancient Greek ἐλεύθερος.

Eleuthero- used in botanical compounds: eleutheropetalous, eleutherophyllous and eleutherosepalous – having the petals, leaves, sepals distinct.

libr- , *liber* book, believed to be a use of liber, the inner bark of exogens.
      (*Oxford English Dictionary*)

*

Solomon Northup was a woodworker. A lumberjack and carpenter, the skills that earned his keep in the North became his punishment in the South.

He was hanged from a tree, and he witnessed other slaves thus hanged. In a glade in the Ayovelles woods, he met a Chickasaw band and heard their music's freedom.

A talented musician, his violin was first his voice and later – its beauty abused by his owner – so much splintered waste. Attempting to make himself heard, he pilfered paper and split a branch to make a pen.

The liberties and limits of wood run through his memoir, *12 Years a Slave*. In Steve McQueen's film adaptation, it is with wood in his skilled hands that Northup convinces a white man of his humanity. Strange fruit borne by Southern trees.

*

Liberty. Librotree.

The Romans believed that bark, peeled in strips, was the first writing material. It's a strange twist of history that we now have books made of wood pulp, which retain the arboreal vocabulary of 'leaves' in their construction.

*

In the Ancient Near East, the phrase 'by tree and stone' meant 'the old ways,' the remembered sources of meaning and oracular speech. Before there were books, there were trees.

> Once upon a time trees were temples of the deities... The different kinds of tree are kept perpetually dedicated to their own divinities, for instance... the bay to Apollo.
> (Pliny the Elder, *Natural History* XII)

Trees were sanctuary: many temples to the Olympian pantheon had groves of trees around them, and archaeologists agree with Pliny that once the trees themselves were the temples.

No wonder Daphne fled into the trees.

*

The myth of Daphne's flight from the god Apollo is one of the best-known Greek myths – but there are no literary sources for it before Ovid's *Metamorphoses*.

Apollo chases, intent on rape: Daphne flees. At the last possible moment, her father Peneus, a river god, hears her cries and turns her into a tree: the laurel, which took her name.

Hearing Peneus mourn, Apollo repents, and swears the laurel will remain sacred to him forever. The use of laurel to make wreaths gives *laureate*.

In Hebrew, Daphna is a name meaning laurel, but also victory.

*

Victory is why Ovid is telling the story. Apollo has just founded the Pythian Games, where singers and musicians would compete to sing his praises. They marked Apollo's victory over the Pythia, a female serpent created by Earth, Gē, after the Flood.

The Pythian Games took place at Delphi, Apollo's major shrine, known as *omphalos*, the navel of the world.

*

There's another story about Daphne and Delphi. Pausanias says that:
> in earliest times the oracular seat belonged to Gē, who appointed as prophetess Daphnis, one of the Nymphai of Parnassus.

(*Description of Greece* 10.5.5, translated by W.H.S. Jones).

*

Diodorus says that Daphne became the priestess at Delphi by another means: the daughter of the seer Tiresias, she was taken prisoner with her sister Manto when the Epigoni sacked Thebes, after the events related in Sophocles' Theban plays. Manto means 'seer', and Apollodorus says she is the mother, by Apollo, of the mythic seer Mopsus.

In some versions, there is only one daughter; in some (mirroring Oedipus and his daughters) two. Manto – the seer; Daphne – the laurel. One to bring the leaves; one to read them.

*

A snake, a tree, a woman, a male god: it's uncannily familiar, although the elements are rearranged as in a dream.

Across the ancient Near East, archaeologists find clay figures of women holding snakes, and evidence that, even in classical Greece, female seers burned leaves to give themselves visions. The snake, the tree, the woman: the old ways.

*

There are two sisters, taken captive in a war. They have lived through terrible events at Thebes. They know there is no safety, only precarity. Each chooses what she understands (understanding the risks) as freedom.

Manto, fathered by Tiresias the seer of Thebes, works with the new regime; tries to change it from within. Daphne, mothered by Tiresias the outlaw, takes to the trees.

*

'On wilds, and woods, she fixes her desire.'

*

Bay laurel (laurus nobilis) is native to the Mediterranean Basin and the Black Sea. In the Miocene, laurel forests fringed the entire Mediterranean: the sacred stands of laurels around shrines such as Delphi are remnants from before the Ice Age.

Laurel is as old as stone; it was there before the Flood.

*

Ovid was banished to Tomis, in the wilds, and woods, of Dacia on the shore of the Black Sea (in modern Romania), in 8 CE, the same year the *Metamorphoses* was finished. Ovid wrote that the reason for his exile was *carmen et error*, 'a poem and a mistake.'

Metamorphoses celebrates, through a narrative of the world from its creation, the Pythagorean belief in mutability. It's a subversive manifesto with a simple slogan:

>Everything changes.

That's not something an emperor, or an empire, wants to hear.

*

Like Augustus, Apollo was a patron of the arts only insofar as they praised him. The laurel wreath is a reward for preserving the status quo.

But it's also a reminder of Daphne inside the tree – of the one who got away, who refused the god and his 'yoke.' Friedrich Nietzsche, drawing on the poet Friedrich Hölderlin, praised the Dionysiac impulse in art – chaotic, ecstatic – over Apollonian individuality and rationality.

What if there's a way between?

*

There's a third story about Daphne, told by Pausanias. Apollo wasn't the first to desire Daphne. Leukippos, a prince of Pisa, disguised himself as a woman and asked to join her band of hunters; she accepted him. But Apollo was jealous, and inspired Daphne and her band to want to bathe. When Leukippos' deception was revealed, Daphne's hunters tore him to death.

Traces of Artemis and Actaeon; Pausanius says that Daphne was dedicated to Artemis, and in his account it's Artemis (Apollo's sister) who turns her sacred virgin into a tree. Daphne, the laurel, is an aspect of Artemis, goddess of wooded high places. And Artemis might be the alternative we need.

*

A girl becomes a tree just like that – but what is a tree? It's Artemisian: a green pause, a way out of the conundrum of serving the state or being destroyed. A way of speaking *with* the world not apart from it.

What if Daphne was a tree *before* she was a girl? Or a treegirl, shapeshifter. To the male gods, girls and trees are only valuable insofar as they can be stripped. But in the old ways, trees are people, too.

*

At the end of her too-short career, the Cuban-American artist Ana Mendieta started working with amate, bark paper, widely used by indigenous Americans throughout their long history. It was the source of a new aesthetic freedom.

In her earlier work, the Silhuetas series, Mendieta disappears into the earth, leaving only the outline of her body. In her later work, she was instead drawing the outline of leaves, finding the tree in the paper. These amategrams often had names in Taino, the indigenous language of Cuba, such as Itiba Cuhababa, Old Mother Blood.

*

When I think about liberty, I think not about leaving, but what is left – what is set free by surviving. I think about the survival of Mendieta in her work, of the tree in the paper, of the girl in the tree.

The choice Daphne made *in extremis* is ours as writers: speak for and with the status quo, or protest and risk transgression. Risk the elision of your history, from priestess of Gē to prisoner of war to pinup girl to plant matter in a world that cannot, and will not, hear the trees.

*

It's 23rd December, 2013. Maria Alyokhina and Nadezdha Tolokonnikova, members of artist-activists Pussy Riot, have both been released from prison, where they should never have been, under a general Russian amnesty for political prisoners.

Like the Greenpeace activists released under the same amnesty, Pussy Riot have protested on environmental issues, trying to prevent deforestation in the Krasnodar region. For them, the rights of women, LGBTQ people, other marginalised groups, and trees go together: they are vulnerable to power because it knows they are free.

*

> We are freer than all those who sit opposite us on the side of the prosecutor, because we can say what we please and we do.
>
> (Nadezhda Tolokonnikova, 8 August 2012, translated by Sasha Dugdale)

*

Līber (freedom) and liber (bark, book) have nothing in common, etymologically or mythologically.

The god forces you into the cage of branches.

The courage of Daphne's choice is believing in the tree: taking hold of bark and branch, sap, leaf, and gall, and speaking through them, an oracle in the tree we have to free ourselves to hear, or be.

AMISS

These running days it's all my Artemis
prosthesis. Her princess dress
refusal puzzled Zeus: tunic,
leggings, boots or barefoot.
Wouldn't catch her with no quiver.
My friend Shelagh, the archer, I wear her
armguard, hard
about these writing fingers & their aches.

Phylactery or Katniss, this
tefillin Barbie lacks what discipline
begins at fingertip, runs zipwire tree- to
treetop, corpuscle on corpuscle
hangs as fire :: constant
oscillation, a hunt for nothing –
for the nothing that hangs it all
together. Dream, then, of a collider

that slide of the bowstring, dance
of the target. All those perfects. Moving
towards what's moving, still
of it: pelvic girdle is the rim
of a bowl and singing (water-filled
and fingertip again, callused
by the press of letters, such alphabets
engendered [where a is for girl

{such curves} and x is for the invisible
invisible, its power], tangential
from the need to move the pencil
point against the heart, the pulse point
on my palm that can't shut up).
Gulp. Blood stutter. And the run again — or
stumble, rather, damn skin unlimiting

against diurnal, sodden blur. It's all:
forgetting what I have forgotten in
cold fingerjoints that yearn, fumbling, for focus,

for the words to – even – name
a calm and grace. Her high, unpeopled
places. Her weather eye. Her absolutely
in-between.

FIONA TAN'S SAINT SEBASTIAN (2001)
    a film 'inquir[y into]... the Toyisha archery festival in Japan, where young girls perform a highly stylised archery contest as a rite of passage into adulthood.'
                        ADRIAN SEARLE, *The Guardian*, 7 October 2004

her lash the arrow
   curved brow echoes
      arm bent at the elbow
         cello her neck

              this is the bow
                 not hair-looped but O
                    opened to show
                       the arch of the archer
                                            fighting back
                   from nail to tongue tip
                 pressed against pressed lip
              say flêche and the pun trips
               the string as it cracks

     its sings of the shadow:
    the film of the photo
  grained silver and lightslow
nothing of lack

VAGINA

She'd always thought it was an alien word, and now it was. What they said, again again, lip-synching to the rhythm of our oldest fear on every screen. Three classical syllables, the feminine rhyme apparently asking, 'Take me to your queen.'

But no salve. No. This was no Churchillian V-sign flicked up to mark a new world, heaven here on earth. There was nothing new when it began: as old as caves.

Or universe. Vastness is one translation, the envelope sheathing and unsheathing cosmic volume. Revealing our vulnerability as theirs. Kristeva, *Black Sun*, chapter and verse: *the speech of the depressed is to them like an alien skin.*

Shed.

She'd shrug it pinkly off, its inner velvet. She's always been. And been here, a Venusian Pirate Jenny slowly amassing the voltage to bring them, across the volutes and inversions of interstellar space, converging in.

AFTER HYPATIA

> What we glimpse of her now is less
> than the frozen trickle of light from a star
> extinct since the Pharaoh's age
>
> yet flickering
>
>   Steven Heighton, 'Rewriting the Dead'

What we glimpse of her now is less
than flesh, her reflection sometime shadowed
on her sister-moon: yet a glimpse is not invisible,
she's there when we register no god more
than the frozen trickle of light from a star,
dreaming all the star has seen in
planes, parabolas ellipsing closer
than a lover gone into their own dreams
where we cannot follow, mysterious as glyphs
extinct since the Pharaoh's age,
that can be read (or so we're told)
propelled as starlight across time,
and so make a world electric
in its charge (as hers) to question
everything

yet flickering.
Between absolutes, she balanced
knowing and uncertainty, circling
bright emptinesses
yet flickering
within her sleepless mind. And in that
uncircled starry open, her flame
met violent fires
yet flickering
across our skies. Light years
after her cold death, a strange fulfillment
for her thoughts starspeed
yet flickering.

ANGRIA

1.

Reader, I did not
marry him. & my sister Catherine
did not die; Lucy, our third, did not stand & wait.

Please, Bella Swan, stop dreaming
of us in our dead gowns & wan.
We haunt you when you make of us ghosts.

2.

At back of the North Wind,
a door. Fallen dolmen, high table
of the witches' sabbat, giantess' childbed.

We lifted it, Antoinette and I, on one secret flight
across the furze. Our rehearsals. I had read all
the bloody plays, knew the day would come: Choose.

Choose father, church and state, be *kindly* called.
Oh heavy stone. Stone in our mouth, stone
our hearts. We did not give in.

3.

The door under the hill
opens on stone. Flags, a passageway,
the scratch (needle, knife, pen). Our Fates,

wyrd daughters of Angria, their land
of wild childmind turned neat and sharp,
cutting us in the compass

of their lives.
Snipsnip. We
didn't have much time.

   4.

The door opens. That's what it's for. & we opened
it & opened until, in passing, we became ourselves
passage. Ghast, hag, bump in the: all the old

names they call us. Wuther. No matter. We are, we
are warning. We are your door: step through us,
furious, onto bare bracken, where the wind

in its raging
is our word
& yours.

PISSING INTO THE WIND: 2004

> This is how one pictures the angel of history.
> WALTER BENJAMIN, 'Theses on the Philosophy of History,'
> trans. Harry Zohn.

pissing into the wind
pissing into release the detrusor muscle and the midbrain's
    periaqueductal gray
pissing into lichen, which is fjallagrasa, into lava and lady's
    bedstraw
pissing into bare arse, into the hiss of the moss, into mosquito
    larvae
pissing into basalt, black obsidian, rolling thufur
pissing into geysirs, into Gulfoss, into oxidised calderas
pissing into the central highlands, a 1 in 2 incline, into
    geothermal steam, into hydroelectric
pissing into tented protests against smelters
pissing into the milkbottle taste of stale aluminium
pissing into fault lines, into the continental divide, into
    volcanic chains
pissing into Midsummer's Eve under the midnight sun
pissing into extinction the Po'uli
pissing into the houses of the elves
pissing into fantasy the plumed horsemen wheeling towards
    lava-landscapes of war
pissing into the coffin of George Patton from the firefields of
    Fallujah
pissing into the dossier, the donut box, the ballot box, the
    history books
pissing into panties reading my cherry for Kerry, reading axis
    of Eve
pissing into evanescence the transit of Venus and the victory
    of Greece
pissing into that dress / I'm going out dancing / Starting off red
    / Clean and sparkling
pissing into the post box, into the ether, into the phone line,

>   into the check-in line
> pissing into winged ink and Chrystos and turquoise and that
>   lost, last transparency
> pissing into the dark against danced silence, floorboards
>   sprung to insistence
> pissing into your ear, pissing into your mouth, pissing into my
>   lips, into my bed
> pissing into the earthquake
> pissing out the tsunami

OSTRAKOI

Sea-secret, once, in our marshy beds & now –
you pick-axe crackers of cunt psephology strike rich
with middens written right through in his name,
our half-shells shattered on his granite

>*as you dance the tarantella*
>*of the castanet dentata*

to jag and fragment. Argument: that we are cast
as pearls before swine every time you prise
us open. We can be poison (saline, iodine), we
can be rough to the touch. Fuck your salt

>*when you dance the tarantella*
>*of the castanet dentata*

and your shallots and your reductions, your lipsmacking
gastro-fascism that would swallow us
whole with a slip of the tongue. We are not yours
to be eaten. We will be (when you're gone) what remains.

>*and we dance the tarantella*
>*of the castanet dentata*

ALL ABOUT SUFFRAGE WAS TAUGHT UNDER MRS. CATT'S DIRECTION

OR, DJUNA BARNES REPORTS FROM THE TRIAL OF PUSSY RIOT.

I've come from the side of the world. I've been on the underside of the watch. I've been breast-to-breast with the ticks.

> Even the air in Russia causes pain to us!
> This is what happens when you touch an abscess ready to burst!
> You struck against the very snakes' nest which has now attacked you!

Glimpses in the Condensed Course of Two Weeks, where all about suffrage was taught under Mrs. Catt's direction.

> When I am powerless, I am strong.
> We are against Putin's chaos.
> Orthodox culture might also be on the side of civil revolt.

Girls who grew old in a year.

> Only when they weighed up the political and symbolic damage that we had inflicted with our art did they decide to protect society against us and our conviction. Prison is Russia in miniature.
> We are freer than all those who sit opposite us on the side of the prosecutor, because we can say what we please, and we do.

The stage was a thing of the future, and future possibilities at work on it: a vivid gehenna!

> That is how this complicated punk adventure ended. Where should the blame lie for the performance in the Christ the Saviour Cathedral and the subsequent trial? It lies with the authoritative nature of the political system.
> I am extremely angered by the phrase 'so-called' which the State Prosecutor uses to refer to contemporary art. This trial is just a so-called trial!

They were not naughty songs, mademoiselle; they were life – They were the little pen knife blade with which one cuts the wrist of malice and deceit.

> Religion was in opposition then.
> They spat on our outstretched hand – They shouldn't have.
> I am not afraid of you.

Oh, dear Lord, what have we done to receive so much beauty per flash!

Note: All offset quotations are from the trial statements made by Maria Alyokhina, Yekaterina Samutsevich, and Nadezhda Tolokonnikova during their trial, as translated by Sasha Dugdale. All other material is quoted from Djuna Barnes' journalism, as collected in ed. Douglas Messerli, *Poe's Mother*.

PENNY FOR THEM

Set mummy free! The liberation cry
of 'The Women's Marseillaise.'
They did try, in May 1914, the suffragettes

unravelling (with axes) those bandages
of patriarchy. Waved as banners. Result!
Women banned from the BM, only welcome

on receipt of a letter from a person
'willing to be responsible for her behaviour.'
A person not her. She is other than

person / responsible. She is the multi-armed
goddess of smash 'n' grab. You shd
see how she uses those beads,

baby. You should see what she does
at quark level. Budding biophysicist
engineering gametes, she is the anti-bomb,

cimota, terracotta, arrow head,
perforated bronze, thiefed sheela-na-gig.
Time to steal them back & that

defaced penny. 'Stamped
with the slogan "votes for
women", it circulated as small

change.'

LONDINOS

Londinos (Celtic): wild

Vote mice. Vote fox. Vote pellet, scuffle, track-stopping
    shadow.
Vote rosebay willowherb, mallow between paving stones,
little mouse-ear, dark mullein. Vote Walbrook, vote Fleet,
vote Effra, vote for wet pencil-traces on the map.
Vote for Mother Red Cap, vote for Mother
Clap! Vote Boudicca, mark your cross for
Boadicea, bringing chariots of Iceni fire. Vote Cornelius,
lately come from Africa to sign his name
to the register of this parish, the year
of our Lord 1593. A vote for Bevis Marks and Princelet
Street resounds the city's hills with the trumpet
of the Lord. Vote for a Durga Puja at the British
Museum, where Rabindranath Tagore once eyed the piratical
thievings. Vote Mary Read, roaring-boy hostage
of Calico Jack. Vote for Margery Jourdain: she can,
or so they say, raise the dead. Vote down
Tyburn tree, vote down the Bailey, ersatz forest
ripe with blasphemous heads shouting treason,
corruption, law's disorder.

Vote with a finger smirred with blackberries
picked beneath the spriggan, tongued patron saint
of abandoned lines. Vote recumbent,
like Oscar, looking up, drunk, in hope
of the stars. Graphite marks the hand that marks the margins,
    overruns the boxes, poised for flight
when the light changes to green.

NO DRAGONS BUT FAIRIES

I am not Masgwid Gloff, first king of Elmet
and I am not Elmet's last bard.
I am not Leeds' spirit of the blitz
nor a royalist, nor a great house.

Not a heritage railway
no model village drinking no beer
nor the stodge of Hovis
or its nostalgia, fake
as Cottingley fairies
as a postcard of Ilkley

but my fingers are caught in woollen mills
and my books come from workers' libraries
and I have long, dark bones
under eyes of pearl
and I have salted away Hockney's
starcast sets ('space,'
he says, 'is more interesting to me
than time') for *The Rake's Progress*

I am a moor, black beetle-browed and calling, calling
I am a golem of beer cans and spliff-ends
upsetting your census, I am an anti-racist
protest and Tina's kids making Mischief Night
I am the undemographic fairy, green on green, coved by
Cloven Hoof Well in Shipley Glen and shimmering
with heathersun, and I am the will o' the wisp spirit
lit window at the Parsonage against the dark,

here comes the girl and her dog
leading you past death into wildness
to those soft, imagined kingdoms

shaped by children in script so small
the page becomes a moorland, unbordered,
& in its weft and carboniferous
warp no passports, no dragons
and no crowns.

WATER-MARGIN

> The sedge has wither'd from the lake;
> And no birds sing.
> JOHN KEATS, 'La Belle Dame Sans Merci'

I live on the sedge. I sing
unseen. It is my song
you do not hear, light as air:
willowdown-dweller, reedwalker.

As a bird I have no country. I sing
there to here. Hear my song:
a 'noisy, rambling warble' on the air,
summerlong singer, water-neighbour.

When winter withers, it's away I sing,
the long length of earth. My song
bends from Arctic to warmer air:
to an Afrikaaner, Europese Vleisanger.

I am citizen of sedge, of sedge I sing;
of the edge, the water-margin. My song
is pidgin, weird Birdish: plucking from air
English, Namlish, Suomi, Oshiwambo, Xhosa.

Shared sound of rain on reeds: I sing
low morning mist. Your songs
condense in mine. I fill the encircling air,
pale loiterer, sedge warbler.

PAS DE DEUX

for Mike and Heather

Entrée

You have always been moving towards and towards.
From out of the north and the west, through orchard and
prairie, running and dancing and longing,
you're come.

Tie the ribbons of your shoes and step out from the wings.

There is no rehearsal, no
Lermontov, no music box. The curtain
is inside your heart and lifts
today. This is the stage, no stage
but what we live, and now –

Adagio

All eyes are on you, loves, all breath
suspended & you dance, hand to tender hand
you hold aloft. And in the perfect stillness, move.

Grand Variation

In such suspension there is iron, dancers know:
muscle and sinew at their long, slow work,
birdlike, burning into flight.

Coda

My more-than-friends: go step by step. Chambered as a heart,
you dance each beat, each breath, each gentle touch.
Together may you find the grace I've found in love.

UNDER THE SAME BLUE SKY

Under the same blue sky, the goddess of Kleifarvatn listens, waits and prepares herself.

She listens.

The fish tell her of fissures; of how we crack to learn our depths. Volcanic heat releases gases, she stresses – but what shapes the earth kills the fishes.

She watches.

She (Eye of Ra) turns the ankh: poison / gift. These elemental surfaces – rock, water, goddess – are process. In the invisible twist of becoming, under the sun. Under the surface, scuba'd into her blood.

She breathes.

The flanks of Krísuvík breathe with her: hot. pain. catch. hale. Earthribs, earthflanks shuddering. Flowing as rock flows; the slowness that overwhelms.

She waits.

What we call the gods are mysteries of scale, the largeness of change accumulated from the infinitesimal. Each cell a Sekhmet: warrior and healer, water and rock.

She turns her skin to the sky.

HOMERIC HYMN TO ARTEMIS

You make a good shadow, says Fox.

She's the goddess of what no longer exists,
the myth of the source,
the clean gulp, the enfilade
leading into the cave
and out. She is there, that
moment in the centre
when the walls fall away and your hands
find themselves in prayer, blades of a labrys
folding closed, this life and its mirror.
She is chevron
wherever it is found: both point and wing,
tip and soft brush past. When I say
she is articulate, I mean in
every joint, in speaking inviolate, say,
or fleet. Antique vocabulation. Chordate,
pathless, reverie. She
is, and is outside, time, moving swifter
than it to grow smaller somewhere
beyond your vision: mote not
molecule. She precedes all, weathers
all in the flicker. Call
her sheet lightning,
heartrace, that arrow
formation taking flight
on the back of your neck late
twilight when — tail flash
between hedges, railings, parked
cars – dark
eyes, she runs beside you
or your shadow,
electron-like, both
there and gone –

She said: I am mathematical. I like
parabolas, she said, Pythagoras. I knew
Hippolyta; later, Hypatia. Each one an
arrow. Not time's but mine. I draw the bow
against those busy calculating
the displacement of air, the vector of kill.

War's no
more than
mathematics,
she said, pencils of geometry
and velocity. Victory to who commands
equations. Who draws with the finest point.
Who stakes the points at A and B and drives
the line that yokes them. But I am

the arc, she said, I demand
calculus. I move on
the cosine, descend
on the oblique, yes,
the arrow that falls on the other side
of the sky. What matters is
to move; to
choose with your compass
eye the path
between two lines and leap
as they collide. Perspective is a lie
told by using the ruler's edge, she says.
In the leap there is
only everything
happening
now

WHERE A = ∞

Artemis runs in a zig-zag. Loop, flicker. Sweat / rain exchange through porous membrane. Above the treeline, under sheet lightning. Goddess of the post apocalypse. Of forage and borage and the return of the wetlands. She shuns the urban but's no farmwife in gingham. Don't ask her on a date. She's *Potnia Theron*, Lady of Wild Things; *Calliste*, Bear-Beautiful. She wins the hunger games because she, hunter, is honed of hunger. Her twin brother, Apollo, he's god of logic and the bright light of day. She is the moon, the crossroads, *limēn*, the gate out of the city, *eileithiya* the loosener, the wind-wise line of the arrow she lets fly. So ask her. Fastness. For (all of) (only) all (of) this.

THE MAYER

> There are no unacceptable sentences, only
> impossible worlds; Einstein has visited Troy
> VERONICA FORREST-THOMPSON, 'It Doesn't
Matter about Mantrippe'

and he unsplit the atom there, under orders from
Marilyn, whom he married, (or was it
Helen), their peace mission ended war
forever, not long after Ziggy Freud
had gone to Thebes, talked Rex Oedipus
out of his neuroses, and earlier
still, Amelia Earhart disappeared
from history to take on the sky
gods, dodging thunderbolts
in her twin-prop plane. Screw
patriarchy, it never happened.
Angela Davis stood at the gates
with her flaming sword and told
D/Zeus and all yall to fuck
right off. That's right, that's Frida
Kahlo in that Mayan frieze, hauling
the princess – with a kiss –
off the altar, her wheelchair
kick-kick-kicking down the ziggurat
of stairs. Won't see her for dust. Elizabeth the First?
In bed with Orlando. She was real, you know:
Virginia Woolf stood in the Ouse and thought,
'Can't do this twice,' climbed into her mind's time
machine, went back and bore
her, Whim Shakespeare's daughterson,
alight with possibility
and dancing. Enter: *Noise and hallowing
as of people a-maying.* No
ribbons, no maypole and no
official yaysay needed: things change all
the time. They change time. Wave

and particle. Stars whose light we see
are farther back than Troy. Before extinctions.
Before oceans. Nothing yet has happened, nothing
has to happen, even what has happened. This is
not real / this is / this is not really
happening. O happy concatenation.
Albus Einstein's particles and Gertrude
Stein's participles: we're given impossibilities,
live this ever-present. (O) dazzle of mayhappening.

BIOGRAPHICAL NOTE

SOPHIE MAYER is a writer, editor and educator. Her poetry has been translated into Russian, Greek, Dutch, and Japanese, and has appeared on poster hoardings in Dublin and as part of Yoko Ono's Meltdown 2013. With Markie Burnhope and Sarah Crewe, she developed the recent wave of UK poetry activism, including the Saboteur Award-winning *Catechism: Poems for Pussy Riot*, *Binders Full of Women*, and *Morning Star* award-winning *Fit to Work: Poets against Atos*. She works with English PEN, and was the Archive of the Now's first Poet in Residence.

Previous collections include *Her Various Scalpels* (Shearsman, 2009), *The Private Parts of Girls* (Salt, 2011), *Kiss Off* (Oystercatcher, 2011) and *signs of the sistership* (with Sarah Crewe, KFS, 2013).

She is a film critic and scholar, author of *The Cinema of Sally Potter*, *Political Animals: The New Feminist Cinema*, and (for the *Oxford Handbook on Contemporary British and Irish Poetry*), 'Cinema Mon Amour', the definitive essay on British poetry and film.

ACKNOWLEDGMENTS

The author wishes to thank to the editors of the following publications, on- and offline, where these poems (or versions of them) first appeared: *Against Rape, The Apple Anthology, Binders Full of Women, Birdbook II, Brand, Catechism: Poems for Pussy Riot, Cimarron Review, Cock No. 7, Collective Brightness: LGBTIQ Poets on Faith, Religion and Spirituality, Fit to Work: Poets Against Atos, Furies, Island Magazine, Joyland Poetry, London Magazine, Morning Star, Oxford Poetry, Poem in Which, Poetry Review, Solidarity Park Poetry: #occupygezi, Strange Horizons, Venus as a Bear, Visual Verse, The Wolf* and *Wordgathering*.

She is grateful to the Hawthornden Foundation for a 2010 Fellowship on which several of these poems were written; to Peter Hughes, for his encouragement to write & permission to reprint 'The Mystique Mutations' from *Kiss Off* (Oystercatcher, 2011); and to first readers Markie Burnhope, Theodoros Chiotis, Facebook (for facilitating), John Kinsella, John McCullough, Katy Price, Angela Rawlings, Shelagh Rowan-Legg, S.F. Said, Preti Taneja and Elizabeth Treadwell.

She is especially grateful to Sarah Crewe: *honnête lectrice, ma semblable, ma sœur*.

Thanks are also due to the following writers and publishers for permission to quote from:
Sasha Dugdale's translation of the Pussy Riot trial transcript for *Modern Poetry in Translation*; Anne Carson's *Agamemnon* in *An Oresteia* (London: Faber & Faber, 2010); Veronica Forrest-Thompson's 'It Doesn't Matter about Mantrippe' in *Collected Poems* (Exeter: Shearsman, 2008); Steven Heighton's 'Rewriting the Dead' in *The Ecstasy of Skeptics* (Toronto: House of Anansi, 1994); John Kinsella's 'Burning Eyes,' in *Armour* (London: Picador, 2011); Douglas Messerli for Djuna Barnes quotations from *Poe's Mother* (Los Angeles: Sun and Moon, 1995).

Selected titles in Arc Publications'
POETRY FROM THE UK / IRELAND include:

Liz Almond
The Shut Drawer
Yelp!

D. M. Black
Claiming Kindred

James Byrne
Blood / Sugar

Jonathan Asser
Outside The All Stars

Donald Atkinson
In Waterlight:
Poems New, Selected & Revised

Elizabeth Barrett
A Dart of Green & Blue

Joanna Boulter
Twenty Four Preludes & Fugues on
Dmitri Shostakovich

Thomas A Clark
The Path to the Sea

Tony Curtis
What Darkness Covers
The Well in the Rain
folk

Julia Darling
Sudden Collapses in Public Places
Apology for Absence

Linda France
You are Her

Katherine Gallagher
Circus-Apprentice
Carnival Edge

Chrissie Gittins
Armature

Richard Gwyn
Sad Giraffe Café

Glyn Hughes
A Year in the Bull-Box

Michael Haslam
The Music Laid Her Songs in Language
A Sinner Saved by Grace
A Cure for Woodness

Michael Hulse
The Secret History
Half-Life

Christopher James
Farewell to the Earth

Brian Johnstone
The Book of Belongings
Dry Stone Work

Joel Lane
Trouble in the Heartland
The Autumn Myth

Herbert Lomas
The Vale of Todmorden
A Casual Knack of Living
COLLECTED POEMS

Pete Morgan
August Light

Michael O'Neill
Wheel
Gangs of Shadow

Mary O'Donnell
The Ark Builders

Ian Pople
An Occasional Lean-to
Saving Spaces

Paul Stubbs
The Icon Maker
The End of the Trial of Man

Lorna Thorpe
A Ghost in My House
Sweet Torture of Breathing

Roisin Tierney
The Spanish-Italian Border

Michelene Wandor
Musica Transalpina
Music of the Prophets
Natural Chemistry

Jackie Wills
Fever Tree
Commandments
Woman's Head as Jug

"The female o, the great hidden opening, is explored, exposed, metamorphosed, eroticized, defiled, queered up, laid out to scrutiny and fantasy in Sophie Mayer's rich collection (O). Sonic and graphic associations as well as torqued literary and mythical references provide the ground for contemporary lessons in seduction, pleasure, brutality, loss and trauma. Under the sign of Louise Bourgeois, Sappho, Butler and other girls, they advocate communal spirit, militancy and revolt as healing tools for love and personal freedom. The result is a sexually polymorphic and culturally meandering book of vows, songs, curses and kisses, complex and stirring pieces from the '(o) in the machine'. Highly recommended."

CAROLINE BERGVALL

"Mayer has created poems that process myth, history and the quotidian in a critical but generative way: they are means of viewing the constraints of language but also offer ways in which it can, in itself, become affirming and liberating. So much of this collection, with its vast erudition, clever language-usage and manipulation of 'the word', is about issues of liberty for one and all. Engage with this and you'll have a unique experience. Mayer is a poet who can draw the threads of human existence together in ways unperceived but wholly essential once you realise they are there. Sappho is back, with metatext. But maybe Sappho *was* metatext, and Mayer knows this."

JOHN KINSELLA

www.arcpublications.co.uk

ISBN 978-1-908376-98-5